the little book of
Shadow Work

*Embracing your shadow is
a powerful act of self-love.*

the little book of
Shadow Work

RICHARD MARTYN

GODSFIELD

An Hachette UK Company
www.hachette.co.uk

First published in Great Britain in 2024 by
Godsfield Press, an imprint of
Octopus Publishing Group Ltd
Carmelite House
50 Victoria Embankment
London EC4Y 0DZ
www.octopusbooks.co.uk

Distributed in the US by
Hachette Book Group
1290 Avenue of the Americas
4th and 5th Floors
New York, NY 10104

Distributed in Canada by
Canadian Manda Group
664 Annette St.
Toronto, Ontario, Canada M6S 2C8

ISBN 978-1-84181-588-6

A CIP catalogue record for this book is
available from the British Library.

Printed and bound in China
10 9 8 7 6 5 4 3 2 1

Commissioning Editor: Louisa Johnson
Designer: Isobel Platt & Hannah Valentine
Assistant Editor: Samina Rahman
Editorial Assistant: Constance Lam
Production Manager: Allison Gonsalves
Illustrations: Bárbara Malagoli

Acknowledgements:
Jan Winter for her encouragement and
skilful editing.
Rod Boothroyd for his help and advice,
especially with the exercises.
Marianne Hill for her support and all
that she has taught me over the years.
My children Alan and Beccy for their
love and support

Contents

Introduction

Shadow work is a powerful and transformative method of life coaching and counselling that supports deep growth and change. It can help anyone who is working through personal issues to heal emotional wounds and overcome negative patterns of behaviour and feeling.

The techniques and exercises in this book are adapted from processes we use in the shadow-work community with our clients. They offer an initial exploration of your shadow, as well as a way to start or continue your personal growth. Shadow work is very effective when it is guided by a qualified practitioner, when you are held securely in a safe space where you can explore vulnerable and difficult territory.

If you have any areas of trauma, or a specific mental health issue which might cause difficulties with the exercises in this book, please be kind and compassionate with yourself and seek professional help and support.

The History of Shadow Work

Shadow work is rooted in the findings of the Swiss psychiatrist Carl Jung in the early 20th century. Jung introduced the concept of the 'shadow' to explain how our unconscious mind holds the parts of our personality we repress or deny. Influential figures, such as the poet Robert Bly, further explored the significance of the shadow, and the importance of acknowledging and integrating these hidden parts of our personality. Today, shadow work has become an increasingly popular and powerful tool for self-discovery and personal growth, drawing both on modern psychology and ancient wisdom.

Getting to Know Your Shadow

Everyone has shadows.
They are part of living.

What is the Shadow?

When we talk about the shadow, we mean our unconscious mind: the part of our mind that is not in our awareness. In psychology, the term 'shadow' refers to those aspects of ourselves that we ignore, deny or suppress.

We are born into the world as complete individuals with all the resources and capabilities we need to survive and thrive, but with no learned knowledge or experience. From that first day, as we grow, learn, experience and develop, we start populating our shadow with lessons we have internalized. These lessons consist of beliefs about ourselves and our place in our family, in our society and culture. In turn, this information affects how we function in the world, operating from a very deep unconscious level within our psyche.

The poet Robert Bly describes this beautifully in *A Little Book on the Human Shadow*. He introduces the metaphorical concept of a 'shadow bag'. Imagine each of us carrying an invisible bag over our shoulder. As we grow up, we put aspects of ourselves that are frowned upon or cause us discomfort into this bag – qualities such as anger, jealousy, vulnerability or even joy and creativity. These repressed characteristics constitute our 'shadow'. Over time, the bag gets heavier, impacting our behaviour and relationships.

As the shadow is held in our unconscious mind, we are not directly aware of what we have put into our bag, though we may have a sense that we are not complete in some way. In shadow work we open this bag, acknowledge its contents, and reintegrate these aspects into our conscious self.

Our shadow holds our deep-rooted beliefs about ourselves, about others, and about the world we live in. This information dictates the way we are, the way we think, the way we feel, the way we behave, the way we are in relationships. It dictates how we are in the world.

How are Our Shadows Formed?

Creating our own shadows is an essential part of how we adapt to the world because, from the day we are born, we hide stuff – both positive and negative aspects of ourselves – in our shadow. It could be anger, the way we express emotion, selfishness, selflessness, playfulness, a sense of fun, a sense of humour, creativity, love, connection... an endless list of energies and qualities.

As infants, the shadow we create is the result of the actions and behaviours of our parents or care-givers. As children, more factors come into the mix, including the behaviours of siblings, other family members, teachers, friends and peer groups, as well as social media, culture and societal expectations as a whole.

We are constantly receiving messages from others, not just through spoken words, but by expressions, actions or even the absence of action. The negative messages tell us that something about us is not accepted or wanted in the family and society in which we are living. In response, we subconsciously deny and suppress that thing, and put it into our shadow. We could receive these messages as the result of a single and sudden shocking event, or as a slow drip of hints and gradual learning.

Consider the following three examples:

- If as a child we were told not to get angry, we may have suppressed our anger and put it into shadow. We might grow up believing we are not an angry person, when, in reality, we have denied our anger.

- If we were told to be quiet all the time, we may have put our ability to express our needs – and our essential communication skills – into shadow, then grown up believing we can't openly communicate our needs.

- If at school we make an effort to paint or write something original and are told that it is no good, or doesn't look like it should, we may internalize a message that we are not creative, good or clever enough. This self-belief will be stored away in our shadow.

How Does the Shadow Affect Our Lives?

What happens to all this stuff we have crammed into our shadow bag? It doesn't just sit there benignly.

As we mature and reach adulthood, we find that what we put into shadow affects how we think and behave. This might show up as issues in our relationships, or in our career, or just feeling not so good about ourselves. The shadow responses to childhood situations were appropriate at the time and indeed kept us safe, but they may not be appropriate to us as adults, and might be holding us back in some way.

If we take the example of our anger being in shadow, put there as a response to pressure not to display childhood anger, we may find that we can't get angry when we need to, or stand up for ourselves. And yet, when we are pushed too far, we may explode with rage, or be passive aggressive or manipulative, to get our way.

Why Work with the Shadow?

When we work with our shadow, we become more aware of the parts of ourselves we have hidden away. By bringing our shadow out into our conscious awareness, we can start to understand ourselves better. It gives us an opportunity to change ourselves by consciously thinking or behaving differently.

Seven benefits of working with your shadow:

• Better confidence and self-esteem

We can believe that we just aren't good enough. By working with our shadow, we can understand where this internal message may have come from, learn to see ourselves more clearly and accept ourselves more fully.

- Improved decision-making

Conflicting thoughts and emotions – often driven by shadowy energies and beliefs – can stall our decision-making, especially when we are under stress. Working with the shadow can help us consciously decide not to heed them, or to come to a more balanced view. Shadow work enables us to operate from a place of greater maturity.

- Increased creativity

The positive aspects of ourselves we put into shadow – inventiveness, creativity, ability to think outside of the box – are equally important. We call these good and positive attributes that we have denied and suppressed our 'Golden Shadow'. Owning our shadow and integrating previously repressed positive energies can enable us to realize and embrace our full potential.

- Better relationships with others

Unconscious projections on to others impact our relationships: we see them through the filter of our shadow, not as they really are. Understanding and taming our projections helps us to see others authentically, and we can be more authentic ourselves. When you learn to fully accept and love yourself, you can fully accept and love others.

- Greater self-acceptance

If we have parts of ourselves in shadow that loathe and criticize us, it is impossible to have full self-acceptance and self-love. By working with the shadow to become aware of these parts, we learn to accept them and take away the influence they have over us. This can lead us to the peace of complete self-acceptance.

- Improved overall wellness

Negative energies and emotions that we suppress into our shadow can show up in any part of the body as aches and pains, or other physical ailments and problems, with no apparent physical cause. Working with your shadow can release negative energy and help you feel better overall.

- More compassion

By working with our shadow, we are less likely to be triggered by the personality traits and behaviours of others. This in turn can help us feel more compassionate towards others and let go of bitter resentments and painful feelings.

How Do I Know
What's in My Shadow?

By its very definition, what we hold in shadow is
unconscious to us: we are not directly aware of it.
But the shadow does leave clues for us to follow.
Here are few ways to find out what might be in
shadow for you.

What do I judge in others?

What traits and qualities of others really irritate and annoy you, or make you angry? The things you judge in others could point to an aspect of yourself that you have denied and suppressed.

For example:

As a child you were chastized for being loud and noisy; you may have been told you were too big for your boots. As a result, you put your ability to shine and promote yourself into shadow. As an adult, you find that you are very annoyed by people you consider to be loud show-offs, and notice that it annoys you far more than it does others. Your reaction mirrors your self-belief that this behaviour is not acceptable. By understanding this, you are less likely to judge other people for the trait, and may let yourself be more confident too.

What do I admire in others?

Why do you put others on a pedestal? Do you ever wish you had their qualities yourself? If so, you may have put that aspect of yourself into your Golden Shadow (see page 85).

If you admire someone who can speak to a large meeting and believe you can't be like that yourself, there is a good chance you have put this ability into your Golden Shadow. It might be that when you were young, at home or at school, when you tried to speak up, you weren't listened to. Your unconscious reaction was to put that ability into shadow. You might tell yourself, 'I could never do that,' or 'I'm not good enough'. Identifying such negative self-talk may help you to overcome the belief and take the first steps to public speaking yourself.

What triggers me?

When we are acting from our shadow, it's as if we are being controlled by unseen forces outside ourselves. In a sense that is true. We are being controlled by shadow energies that we are mostly unaware of, and unable to consciously control, but which can come out suddenly in response to interactions or events.

Something causes you to have an immediate emotional response, such as anger or fear. Afterwards, you realize your response was disproportionate and felt alien, or out of character. It feels as though you couldn't help yourself, and had no control. This can be destabilizing. There will probably be a historical pattern of you responding this way to similar events and identifying it will help to avoid future outbursts.

What do I do compulsively?

What are your compulsive behaviours? Or has a compulsion become an addiction? In the shadow-work community, we believe compulsive or addictive behaviours are a symptom of a suppressed need for connection, nurturing or comfort, that was not met in our childhood. It is a soothing response to the pain of a childhood trauma.

Well-known behaviours that fit into this category are drinking, smoking, over-eating or drugs, but you might well be compulsively cleaning, checking the door is double-locked six times before you go to bed... anything that you do repeatedly and you can't stop or control. Exploring your shadow and facing this pain or absence can be a helpful step to tackling the addiction or behaviour.

What do I feel in my body?

Very often our face and body language betrays our unknown feelings, but we can be completely unaware of it until someone else notices and comments.

Someone might say in passing, 'Cheer up, it may never happen,' and yet you were not aware your face and body language had signalled you were feeling sad. Feelings and emotions that are suppressed in our shadow can often show up as a symptom in our body; a pain, a tightness, a tingling feeling, they can manifest in many different ways. The symptoms can often be relieved by revealing the shadow energies that lie behind them.

EXERCISE:
What's in My Shadow?

Over the page, you will learn about
journaling: a useful tool. In your journal,
explore what might be in your shadow, using
the following prompts. Be open, curious
and honest with yourself. It is not easy to
recognize shadow qualities in ourselves that
we have denied, sometimes for decades. At
first it may seem that only a few of your most
obvious shadows are revealed, but as you
continue with your shadow-work journey
and become more aware, more will
become apparent.

- Focus on people you judge or dislike. What qualities or traits do you judge or dislike? Have you ever, now or in the past, behaved like that? What do you believe about yourself in respect to these behaviours? Is it possible you have put this behaviour into shadow? If so, what childhood experience caused you to do that?

- Bring to mind someone you admire or envy. What qualities or traits do you admire or envy? What do you believe about yourself in respect to these behaviours? Is it possible you have put this behaviour into shadow? If so, what childhood experience caused you to do that?

- Remember the last time you were triggered to an emotional reaction. What happened to cause it? With hindsight, was your reaction disproportionate? How do you feel about the way you reacted: did it feel out of character? Did you have control over your emotions? Is it possible you have put this behaviour into shadow? If so, what childhood experience caused you to do that?

- Can you identify any compulsive behaviours or addictions? What impact do they have on your life? Have you tried to control them, and, if so, how difficult are they to control? How might this behaviour be soothing you, and what childhood pain might it be soothing?

Working with Your Shadow

'We see the world not as it is, but as we are'

STEPHEN COVEY,
ANAÏS NIN ET AL

Tools for Working with Your Shadow

Here are some useful tools you can use to access your shadow and work with it. As with any tool, it takes practice to be able to use them well. For all of them, prepare a space where you can be alone and comfortable. You might not find it easy to use all the tools at first, but just experiment and use those that work for you, in a way that works for you.

Journaling

Regular journaling is an effective technique for self-reflection. Write down all the emotions you are feeling; any sensations in your body; any event that has triggered those emotions and sensations; your thoughts in response to those emotions and sensations; anything you are grateful for; any plans or goals for the day. In the journaling exercises in this book, I give you prompts. These aren't questions you *have* to answer, they are just guides to direct your thinking and self-reflection.

Meditation

In our daily lives, our minds can be very busy, with a heavy traffic of fast-moving thoughts. Meditation is a powerful technique for slowing down the mind and becoming more aware of our thoughts. Cultivating this practice can help us to mentally note them, and become more aware of the influence of our shadow on our thinking.

Visualization

Imagining yourself in a situation you desire and following a story or journey in your mind to get there is a powerful way to explore aspects of yourself. Some take to this more than others, but if you can embrace and practise visualization, you can not only reveal your shadow, but also bring healing to parts of yourself that need it.

EXERCISE:
Setting Your Intention

Shadow work is more effective when you have identified a good reason to take the journey, so before exploring your shadow, think about what you would like to achieve. Take up your journal and write a statement of intent. This statement can be whatever you like, but it's useful to follow a two-part sentence structure:

- What it is you wish to change or understand about yourself in your life right now: 'I want to…'

- Describe how this change would affect your life now and in the future '…so that I can…'

Working with Parts of Ourselves

In shadow work, we use the idea that we are made up of many psychological parts.

This idea is based on the understanding that our personality is not a single, unified entity, but rather a complex system of various sub-personalities, each with its own perspectives, feelings, memories and motivations.

This can be very confusing, as often the different parts within ourselves work against each other. The parts can manifest themselves within us in different ways. At times we may think, behave, stand, walk or speak differently, or even appear as ourselves at different ages. Recognizing parts of ourselves, and listening carefully to them, can help lead us to our shadow.

EXERCISE:
Listening for Parts of Yourself

———————

We often think and talk in parts, without realizing: 'I'm in two minds about that!' or 'On the one hand… and on the other hand…' So here is a simple exercise to begin to identify those different parts of yourself. Approach it with a sense of curiosity and compassion.

If you encounter resistance or fear, or a judgement or criticism coming up, just acknowledge it, and try to accept this is just a fearful or judging part of you. Listen carefully to the fearful part, as it might mean that this exercise isn't right for you at this moment.

It takes practice to be able to identify different parts of yourself. On some days, or with certain issues, some parts of you will be louder than others.

- Sit in a comfortable and quiet place, where you will not be disturbed.

- Take a few deep slow breaths to relax your body and mind.

- Bring a recent issue to mind, where there is some internal conflict or emotion for you.

- Try and identify different parts of you that have separate thoughts or feelings on the issue. For example, you might feel excited and afraid at the same time. One part might want to follow a particular course of action, another part might want to do the opposite.

- Make a simple note of the parts you notice in your journal.

Characterizing Parts
of Ourselves

In shadow work, we use symbols to represent and characterize the different parts of ourselves. When we have identified a specific part, we can use a prop to represent it. This can be anything: a soft toy, an ornament, a piece of clothing; as long as it feels right for you.

It can also be helpful to place the props in a dedicated space. You can use any surface, a carpet, a defined area on the floor, a table, a bed. As long as you can place your props on it, it doesn't matter. Experiment and see what works for you.

When you want to work with a particular part of yourself, you can step into and inhabit the energy of that part of you. You can do this by holding the prop or wearing the clothing. Let all other parts of you fade into the background and fully inhabit the energy of the part you are exploring. It might help you to close your eyes to do this.

EXERCISE:
Speaking from the Emotions

Here, we look at parts of ourselves that represent the main emotions: grief, anger, fear and joy. Grief includes sadness in varying degrees; anger includes being annoyed or irritated; fear includes anxiety; joy includes happiness and contentment. Shame and guilt are common emotions, however, in shadow work, we think of them both as fears. Shame is a fear that we are wrong or bad in some way. Guilt is a fear that we have done wrong to others.

Bring to mind a recent issue or event that may have disturbed you in some way. Write a sentence or two from the parts of yourself as guided below.

- From any part that feels sadness

- From any part that feels anger

- From any part that feels fear

- From any part that feels shame or guilt

- From any part that feels joy

- Which parts are the loudest?

- Which parts are the quietest?

- Which parts would you like to hear less from?

- Which parts would you like to hear more from?

Projections and Transference

Projection

Projection is an unconscious psychological mechanism in which we attribute the emotions, beliefs, impulses and thoughts that we have suppressed and put into our shadow on to someone else. It is a defence mechanism: we defend ourselves against these unwanted feelings by denying them and putting them into shadow. However, these feelings do not stay hidden forever: we externalize them when we unconsciously project them.

Every day, we see in others what we can't see in ourselves. But this can be a distortion of reality: if we view others through the clouded lens of our own shadow, we don't see them as they truly are. Shadow work can help improve our relationships by clearing away the shadow obscuring our view of other people.

The projection of our shadow on to others has major implications for our relationships, as it can lead to misunderstandings and conflict. If you can be open and honest with your self-enquiry, spotting what you project on to others is a clue about what you have put into shadow.

Transference

Transference is a particular form of projection, where we subconsciously see another person as a significant figure from our past. This is commonly a parent or a family member, but it could be anyone. We then react to the person from the present as if they are this historical figure. For example, a man might see large elements of his mother in his girlfriend. He is viewing her like that because he is projecting and transferring those elements of his mother on to her. Regardless of whether these perceived traits are positive or negative aspects of his mother, naturally, this transference could create difficulties in their relationship.

EXERCISE:
Understanding Your Projection

Think of a person you have a current issue or conflict with. Perhaps they have upset or angered you in some way, and the relationship that has become challenging.

- Choose a prop, perhaps a coloured cloth, to represent them, and place the prop on a work space that you can sit by, wherever it feels right.

- Sit back in your seat and think of what messages you get from this person. These aren't words that have been spoken, but what you sense from interacting with them. They might be conveyed by just a look, or through body language.
  On a large blank piece of paper, write the messages you get from this person, in writing clear enough to read when the paper is placed in your work space and you sit back in your seat.

- Rephrase the messages so that they reveal something about you, then write them down on the paper. For example, if the message on the paper from the other person was, 'I am superior to you,' your rephrasing of it might be, 'You are inferior to me.'

- Place the paper with the messages on the prop, sit back in your seat and look at them. Notice how you feel. Which of your different parts are alive for you? An angry part, a sad part, or any other part?

- Ask yourself the following questions: Have you heard these messages before from anyone else? Do you tell yourself similar messages, or think about yourself in this way? Do you ever say these things to anyone else? When was the first time you can remember hearing these messages? Might these messages live inside you, in your shadow?

- Reflect on this exercise in your journal.

Meeting Your Inner Child and Adult

Even inside the womb, our experiences start to shape and mould the person we are to become.

Connecting with
Your Inner Child

In shadow work, we use the term 'Inner Child' to refer to the part of us that still carries the emotions and feelings from our childhood, and the beliefs about ourselves that we adopted at different stages of our development.

As most of our shadow was formed in childhood, being able to access and connect with our Inner Child is a very powerful way of revealing our shadows and working with them. In shadow-work terms, we are busy stuffing our shadow bag from birth right up to our late 20s. You may have several Inner Children of different ages, for example, an infant, a teenager and a young adult.

Please be aware that while carrying out this work you may experience intense emotions and unearth difficult memories. Please approach these exercises with caution, kindness and patience, and seek the support of people you trust.

Attachment theory

Developed by psychologist John Bowlby, attachment theory explains how the relationship between infants and their primary care-givers shapes their emotional and social development. It starts from the basis that children are biologically predisposed to form attachments with care-givers as a means of survival.

Secure attachment, where care-givers are responsive and sensitive to a child's needs, leads to positive outcomes, such as emotional resilience and healthy relationships in adulthood. In contrast, insecure attachments, which arise from inconsistent or neglectful care-giving, can result in emotional difficulties and relationship issues.

The theory emphasizes the critical role early experiences with care-givers can play in shaping an individual's behaviour and personality development throughout life.

EXERCISE:
Inner Child Journaling

Find a comfortable, warm and quiet place where you won't be disturbed. It might help to have a picture of you as a child to hand, or an object that reminds you of your childhood. Relax yourself by taking a few deep and slow breaths. Write in your journal, using the following prompts to guide you, but writing freely. Or you may prefer just to speak to the prompts, then summarize them in your journal afterwards.

- What do you know about your birth and the earliest years of your life?

- What is your earliest memory?

- What comes up for you when you remember this?

- Bring to mind your childhood memories of your mother, father or care-givers, the bad memories as well as the good.

- Describe your connection with each person you think of, using one-word adjectives such as 'close', 'distant', 'loving', 'anxious' and so on.

- Were other family members important to you?

- Bring to mind another significant event in your childhood. How old were you at this time?

- If you had siblings, what was your relationship with them like?

- What was your experience of early or later school?

- How were your friendships throughout your childhood?

- What significant memories do you have from your teenage years?

EXERCISE:
Inner Child Visualization

Begin by finding a quiet and comfortable place where you won't be disturbed. Sit or lie down in a relaxed position.

If you wish, choose a prop to represent your Inner Child. Ideally this would be something you can hold or hug while you are visualizing, such as a soft toy or a cushion.

- Close your eyes and take a few deep breaths: inhale slowly through your nose, hold for a moment, then exhale gently through your mouth. With each breath, allow your body to relax more deeply.

- In your mind, visualize a safe, peaceful place. This could be somewhere you've been before, a scene from nature, or anywhere that feels secure and comforting. Notice the details of this place: the colours, sounds and smells.

- In this safe space, imagine your Inner Child appearing. This might be you at a specific age, or a more general youthful version of yourself. Observe your Inner Child: their appearance, expressions and demeanour.

- Take a moment to simply observe your Inner Child. How do they seem to feel? Are they happy, scared, curious? Remember, there's no need to force a conversation; just being present with your Inner Child is powerful.

- If it feels right, you might want to ask your Inner Child if they want anything from you, or if they have anything they want to tell you. What do they want most of all? Listen with an open heart and mind. Respond with kindness, understanding and reassurance.

- You might visualize yourself offering a gesture of comfort to your Inner Child, such as a hug, holding hands or simply sitting together. Assure your Inner Child that they are safe, cherished, loved and valued.

- When you feel the visualization is complete and it's time for you to leave your Inner Child, thank them for being with you, and promise to return and be with them again.

- Gently bring your attention back to your current surroundings. Wiggle your fingers and toes, take a deep breath, and finally open your eyes.

- After the exercise, you might find it beneficial to journal about your experience. Write down any feelings, insights or messages that came up during your visualization. Write down what you think your Inner Child wanted most of all, and reflect on what you might be able to offer to them.

- Imagine how your Inner Child lives inside you. How can you connect with them again in future? Now that you've met them, is there a prop, picture, memory or feeling you can invoke to help you to reconnect to them?

- If you can't feel any love or connection with your Inner Child, it may be that another part of you is preventing this from happening. It could be a critical, fearful or protective part of you.

Connecting with Your Inner Adult

Our Inner Adult is the version of us who can act responsibly in the world, who holds adult qualities such as compassion, calmness, vision, sound judgement, nurturing, wisdom and care. The Inner Adult is our internal leader, it knows who we are, and where we are going in our life. It can be a good parent and can make good conscious decisions, being logical and rational. It is also the part of us that can self-regulate emotions, and it is the part of us that knows we are good enough and has confidence in us.

In some of us, this part can be underdeveloped or dormant, so we don't have access to this internal resource when we need it. The Inner Adult develops in us as we grow, from infancy, through childhood and the teenage years, to being an adult in the world. But it can be wounded along the way, with internal messages such as, 'I am not good enough,' 'I can't be seen or heard,' or 'I am bad,' that knock our self-belief.

When our Inner Adult is healthy and showing up fully in our lives, we can have a sense of being at peace in our own skin, and in touch with our inner happiness and joy.

In shadow work, the Inner Adult is very useful and powerful. We can use it to support us when we are working with difficult or painful aspects of ourselves.

EXERCISE:
Inner Adult Journaling

This journaling exercise helps you to explore
what your Inner Adult may be like for you.
Use the prompts below to guide you.

- Think of someone who embodies the personal
  qualities you think an adult should have. It could
  be family member, a friend, someone who you
  admire, even a fictional character.

- What qualities does your Inner Adult have? You
  may have put these qualities into your shadow, so
  think about any times you may have acted in an
  adult way. Can you recall being complimented?

- Reflect on your goals and how you achieve them.

- Think about a time you had to make a difficult
  decision, how you approached it, and what this
  tells you about your Inner Adult.

- Reflect on your values in life, and how you live
  by your values.

EXERCISE:
Inner Adult Visualization

In this visualization, you can try to imagine your Inner Adult, however they appear for you. This may be a version of you, or it may be another person or character that came to mind in the journaling exercise. It takes practice to develop an awareness and a sense of your Inner Adult, but if you can grow this part of you, it will be a powerful resource to use on your shadow-work journey.

- Find a quiet space where you won't be disturbed.

- Stand up with an upright posture.

- Take a few deep, slow breaths to relax and calm your mind.

- Close your eyes if you wish, go inside yourself, and let all other parts of you fall away.

- Imagine you are in a large space, such as a field, and in the distance you see a figure approaching.

- As the figure draws closer, you recognize it as your adult self, or your ideal adult person. Notice how they carry themselves, how they are dressed, how they look, how you feel about them.

- They now come to stand right in-front of you. Feel their energy and presence. Look into their eyes and connect with them. Try and get a sense of all the qualities this figure has.

- If you feel able to, take a step forward and step right into your adult figure, taking on their energy and power. If you don't feel able to do this, just stay in connection with your adult figure and feel their adult qualities.

- Feel the energy of your adult figure in your body. Where can you feel it in your body? Does it have a colour, shape or texture? Is it still or moving?

- When you feel you have done all you can to connect with and embody this adult energy, open your eyes and bring yourself back to the present. See if you can still retain the feeling of your adult, by anchoring to the feeling in the body you experienced.

- Reflect in your journal what you gained from the experience of this exercise.

If you can't visualize an Inner Adult, or if you get an image you don't like, that is OK. It might be that your Inner Adult qualities are suppressed very deep in your shadow and you can't access them yet, so you may need to work on other aspects of your shadow to uncover your Inner Adult. Be patient and kind to yourself, and recognize this is all part of the learning process.

Exploring Your Sadness and Grief

Grief can be so painful that we often suppress it and try to carry on.

Working with Sadness and Grief

Exploring our sadness and grief can be very vulnerable and painful territory, but it can also be healing to exercise these emotions in a safe place. So only explore this section if you feel you are able, and if you have access to the support you might need.

Grief is our emotional reaction to losing someone we are attached to, or something important to us. We all associate grief with the loss of a dear loved one, but we can also experience grief over the loss of anything we treasure. We can grieve the loss of a job, the loss of our childhood innocence, the loss of money, the loss of security, and so on.

Grief can accompany all the other main emotions as well: anger and fear and maybe even joy. For example, if someone loses a parent they will feel grief, but if that parent had hurt them at a young age, they may also have feelings of anger and fear. In shadow work, we allow – we actively want – ourselves to recognize, express, acknowledge, and welcome all the emotions, so that they are not suppressed in our shadow.

Sadness is a part of grief, as well as a reaction to disappointment or hurt. It's a natural response to situations that are upsetting, hurtful or sorrowful. Sadness can arise from our shadow when triggered by a current situation. When we inhabit the energy of the sad part of us, we can often find that it is a very young part, and that the root of our sadness lies in our childhood experiences.

EXERCISE:
Speaking the Unspoken Words of Grief

This offers you the opportunity to say whatever you want directly to the object of your grief. The exercise has been written from the perspective of grief for a person, but it can also be used for any other grief you feel.

Find a comfortable and quiet space where you will not be disturbed, and you can say whatever you need in private.

You might find it useful to use a prop, or maybe a photograph, to characterize the object of your grief, and place this in a work space. You can connect to the person by holding or touching the characterization of them throughout the exercise.

- Relax yourself with some deep, slow breaths.

- Go inside yourself and try to get in touch with the feelings of loss you have, and then just say whatever you want to say. Try and speak directly to the object of your grief, as if the real person was there. If you are at a loss for words, start with small things: what you miss about them; a memory you have of them and how you felt then; what you found difficult; what you have lost. Just let the words flow. If there are tears, let the tears flow.

- If other emotions arise, such as anger, fear or joy, let those parts speak as well. It might be helpful to represent these other parts with separate props or cloths.

- When you feel you have said enough, just thank them for listening, and say goodbye.

- Settle and relax yourself with some slow breathing. You may want to leave the room and get some fresh air before clearing the props away.

- Reflect and journal on this experience.

EXERCISE:
Working with Sadness

This exercise helps you to connect with the
part of you that feels sadness, so you can
bring some support to that sad part. It is
essentially a re-parenting exercise, helping
you to show yourself care and support when
you need it. You may feel sad or disappointed
around a certain situation or event that has
recently happened in your life, or you may
feel sad and you don't really know why.
In shadow work, we explore directly the
part of us that feels the sadness, to try and
understand the real root of this and the
negative thoughts that accompany it.

Sit in a place where you are comfortable and won't be disturbed.

- Relax yourself with a few deep, slow breaths, breathing in through the nose and out through the mouth.

- Bring to mind a situation around which you feel sadness.

- Represent the part of you that feels sad with an appropriate prop, such as a cloth, and place it in your work space. A soft toy or cushion, something you can hold close to you, is good for this.

- Connect to the sad part of yourself by holding the prop, letting all other parts fall away. Feel into the energy of the sad part. Where do you feel the sadness in your body? What does your body want to do? Do you want to lie down, do you want to curl up? Do whatever your body wants to do.

- Let your sad part speak by noticing how old the part feels. Are there any early sad memories that come to mind? What does this sad part need right now, what does it want most of all?

- Spend as much or as little time as you need in this sad part.

- When you feel ready, place the characterization prop down in the work space and step out of the energy of this sad part.

- Now you have stepped out of this sad part of yourself, you can bring support and comfort to it. To do this, try and connect to the energy and compassion of your Inner Adult (see page 48).

- Hold the prop representing the sad part of yourself, from the perspective of your Inner Adult. Hold it, hug it in an appropriate and comforting way.

- Knowing what this sad part needs from you, speak to it, and tell it whatever it needs to hear. Take your time and really connect, support and nurture the sad part.

- When you feel that you are ready to complete this exercise, put the sad part down in the work space. Come back to the present and the whole of yourself, with all your different parts.

- Reflect on this exercise in your journal. How do you feel now?

Understanding Your Anger

'Holding on to anger is like grasping a hot coal to throw it at someone else; you are the one who gets burned.'

BUDDHA

Working with the Shadow of Anger

Anger is complex and is often perceived as a negative emotion. Many of us lose touch with our anger and suppress it into our shadow. We might think of ourselves as placid people who don't get angry, and we can then act in a passive aggressive way. We may also then have a problem setting and maintaining our boundaries, and find ourselves being taken advantage of. Alternatively, many of us lose control over our anger, and find that it erupts from us suddenly when we're triggered, becoming rage.

Personal boundaries

Personal boundaries help define who we are as individuals, distinguishing our own thoughts, feelings and needs from others. Boundaries allow us to protect ourselves from being overwhelmed by the emotional needs of others, helping us to value, respect and prioritize our own needs and feelings. They help us to build respectful and fulfilling relationships, enabling clear and authentic communication. Overall, they are essential to our development and for our own sense of self-worth.

The emotion of anger can be very useful to help us identify when we need to set boundaries. If we feel angry, it is a sign that our boundaries have been violated. Anger contains a lot of power, but when it erupts from our shadow in an uncontrolled way, it can be harmful. When it is suppressed so effectively that it doesn't show externally, it can turn inward on to ourselves; this can result in us feeling bad or shameful, and can lead to self-harming behaviours. In shadow work, we work with our anger to try to connect with it and understand it in a safe way.

Journaling About Anger

Explore your relationship with anger,
using the prompts below to guide you.
Once you understand your anger, you can
then consciously use its power to set your
boundaries in a clean and assertive way.

- Do you get angry? If you do, what makes you angry?

- Have others ever described you as angry?

- How has your anger affected your life, or how has your lack of anger affected your life?

- Do you have personal boundaries in your life? Consider what is unacceptable to you.

- Who can you say **NO** to? Who can't you say **NO** to, and why?

EXERCISE:

Connect with
Your Anger

In order to understand your anger, it
is important to get in touch with this
emotion and feel its power and energy.
This exercise gives you the opportunity to
act out your anger in a safe space, where it
has no real-world consequences.

Find a private and quiet space where you won't
be disturbed, and at a time when you won't be
overheard. You might want to shout and make a lot
of noise in this exercise.

- Choose a prop or cloth to represent the person
  with whom you are angry and sit in front of it.

- Think of the person, and really bring them to
  your mind.

- Stand up, then 'step in' to the exercise: inhabit the
  energy of this angry part of you.

- Looking at the prop that is the person, bring to
  mind what they have done to make you angry.
  Think about how you feel about what they did.
  Why did it upset you? How angry are you?

- Speak to the person, and let them know how you
  feel about what they did. Don't hold back; you
  can shout, stamp your feet, raise your fist... allow
  yourself to get really worked up.

- When you have got all you need to say out of your system, and you are sure the person has heard and understands how angry you are, stop talking. Put the prop down and step away from it.

- Focus inwards and feel the energy in your body. Where do you feel it in your body? Does it have a colour, a shape or a texture? Do you have a sense about what this energy wants for you, or how it wants to serve you?

If, during this exercise, you found that you couldn't get angry with the object of your anger, ask yourself the following questions to understand if there are any blocks to your anger:

- What are the risks with your anger?

- Is there a part of the object of your anger that you love and don't want to hurt?

- Does the object of your anger have more power than you in this situation?

- Do you find that you need support to stand up for yourself? How might you get this support?

EXERCISE:
Setting Boundaries

This is a way you can practise using your power to set a boundary with someone. If you were able to access your anger in the previous exercise, then you can connect with that energy by remembering how it felt in your body, and its colour, shape and texture. Even if you weren't able to access your anger, you can still practise setting a boundary in an assertive way.

Sit down in a quiet and comfortable space. Relax into the space with a few deep, slow breaths.

- Choose a cloth, prop or object to represent a person with whom you want to set a boundary, and place it on the work space. Choose a distance to stand away from the prop, whatever distance feels right for you.

- Think of the person you would like to set a boundary with. What boundary would you like to set with them? Try and keep it factual, so there is less opportunity for dispute. Also, choose to set a boundary around just one behaviour at a time, as there may be multiple boundaries to set.

- On a blank sheet of paper, write the boundary you wish to set in the format: 'It is not OK with me that you...' This is a clear way of expressing your needs.

- Practise vocalizing this boundary by addressing the prop and repeating the words you have written.

- Now, think about how annoyed or upset you were with the other person, try and get in touch with the anger you felt. Notice where you feel the energy and power of the anger in your body, remember its colour, shape and texture. Try and tap into that energy and power and use it to deliver your message. Say your boundary-setting sentence again using your power. Say it with control, force and determination, but without raising your voice.

- Repeat this a few times, each time trying to control and use the power and energy raised in you. Notice how it feels to say this out loud.

You may find that you can't express your boundary to the other person, and something is blocking you. If that is the case, ask yourself the following questions:

- Is it a risk for you to say this?

- Is there a part of the object of your boundary-setting that you love and don't want to hurt?

- Does the object of your boundary-setting have more power than you in this situation?

- Do you need support to stand up to the other person? How might you get this support?

Exploring Your Fears and Anxieties

'A man that flies from his fear may find that he has only taken a short cut to meet it.'

JRR TOLKIEN

Working with Anxiety and Fear

Fear is an emotional response to a specific and real threat, though we might feel that the amount of fear we have is disproportionate to the threat itself, for instance if we harbour a fear of spiders. Anxiety is an emotional response to a perceived or imagined threat that hasn't yet arrived. The threat may not be identifiable to the conscious mind. There is an overlap between anxiety and fear: anxiety may become fear, or a fear can lead to further anxiety.

In shadow work, we work with parts of us that feel anxious or afraid. They may show up as a hesitancy to do or say something, or as procrastination. We may have learned to behave this way when we were young to protect us from emotional and even physical harm. However, as we become adults, this shadowy safety behaviour might no longer be appropriate as the threats we experienced then no longer exist. Becoming aware of such behaviours offers us the opportunity to change them.

Your Inner Safety Officer

This part of us that keeps us safe is so important in shadow work that we have given it a name. We call it our Safety Officer. There may be more than one Safety Officer, and these may be of different ages. The Safety Officer gives us strategies for keeping us safe, and they are responding in the adult world with a behaviour learned in the child's world.

For example, if as a child we witnessed our parents loudly shouting and arguing and it made us fearful, we might have adopted a response of hiding away rather than confronting our arguing parents. This is the Safety Officer's strategy for coping in this childhood situation, which is then stored in the shadow as our automatic response to confrontation. As an adult, we may find that we actively avoid confrontation, stay quiet and keep out of the way, even in situations where we should speak up and be heard.

Journaling on Risk, Fear and Anxiety

In your journal, you can explore your
anxieties and fears, using the prompts below
to guide you.

- What is my attitude to risk?

- What scares me and what makes me anxious?

- Can I recall the most recent time I felt scared
  or anxious?

- How do I protect myself and keep myself safe in
  these situations?

- Can I recall an earlier time, perhaps in childhood,
  when I felt scared or anxious?

- What fears and anxieties did I experience during
  my childhood?

- What strategies did I learn to keep myself safe in
  my childhood?

EXERCISE:

Exploring Your Anxious and Fearful Part

Go to a quiet place where you won't be disturbed. You can sit or stand to start this exercise.

- Choose a prop or cloth to represent the anxious or fearful part of you.

- Bring to mind a recent situation around which you feel some anxiety. Or bring to mind something you fear.

- Hold the prop, and step into the energy of the anxious part of you. Keep the situation in your mind and notice what you feel in your body.

- When you feel connected to your anxious part, ask yourself the following questions:

1. What is the risk you see in this situation? What might happen?

2. What are you doing to protect yourself from that risk?

3. What is the earliest memory you have of a situation where you felt scared or anxious?

4. What was the risk for you then?

5. What did you do then to try and protect yourself from that risk?

- Can you see any similarity between the way you protected yourself then, and the way you are protecting yourself now?

- When you are finished, put the prop representing the anxious part down and step away from its energy.

- Reflect in your journal what this exercise was like for you, what you may have learned about your anxieties and fears, and your habitual ways of protecting yourself from them.

You can also connect to your Inner Adult (see page 48), and see if that part of you has a different perspective on the situation that makes you anxious. Your Inner Adult may have some advice for your anxious part, and it may be able to support and calm it.

Working with Your Inner Critic

We all have a voice inside us that judges and criticizes us. For some, this voice can be quite friendly and criticize us constructively, but for others, it can be very loud, harsh and judgemental. Our Inner Critic is a part of us that operates from our shadow, based on internalized self-beliefs we adopted from our childhood and earlier life. It can be the internalization of external voices we heard in our developmental years, or it can be a voice we generated inside ourselves in response to situations we experienced.

Our Inner Critic is the source of our negative self-talk and our doubts about our own abilities. It can engender in us an attitude of perfectionism, a fear of failure, a fear of being judged by others, and considerable anxiety generally. As well as judging ourselves, our Inner Critic can also judge others, so we can find ourselves being overly judgemental and harsh about other people.

Your Persecutor

In shadow work, we call our loud and more virulent Inner Critic our Persecutor. Our Persecutor not only judges us and others harshly, but has a desire to punish as well, sometimes in cruel ways. This can show up as sarcasm, putting people down, ridiculing or excluding them. There are many other subtle ways of punishing people.

When our Persecutor turns inwards and punishes us, it can result in us not caring about ourselves, not allowing ourselves to get what we deserve, and possible self-harming behaviours. The Persecutor is not generally acceptable in families or society and is a part that is often suppressed and denied. But this denied Persecutor part can hold a lot of energy. Every part of ourselves exists to serve us in some way, and the Persecutor part exists to give us control and therefore to protect us, but in a very different way to the Safety Officer.

Drama Triangle

The Drama Triangle, conceptualized by Stephen Karpman, is a psychological and social model that maps out dysfunctional interpersonal interactions. It features three roles: Victim, Persecutor and Rescuer. The Victim feels oppressed and helpless, the Persecutor is seen as controlling or critical, and the Rescuer provides unsolicited help or support, often enabling the Victim's sense of powerlessness. These roles are fluid, with individuals shifting between them in various interactions.

The model is used to understand conflict dynamics, highlighting how people can unconsciously play these roles to fulfil psychological needs. Recognizing and breaking free from these patterns can lead to healthier and more empowered interpersonal relationships.

Shame and guilt

Shame and guilt are difficult emotions and they overlap, but they can be defined in this way: guilt is a fear that we have done something wrong or bad, even though we may not be a bad person. Shame is a fear that we *are* bad, that there is something wrong with us. Both emotions are based in fear, and in shadow work we see them as manifestations of our inner Persecutor. If we are feeling shame, there is a part of us that feels ashamed, but also there is an internal part of us that is doing the shaming.

This is a difficult and vulnerable territory and requires a skilled practitioner to hold a safe space to help guide you in this work. However, here is an exercise to help you to explore your Inner Critic and your Persecutor.

Journaling Around Your Inner Critic and Persecutor

Use these journaling prompts to explore your Inner Critic and Persecutor.

- How do you judge others?

- How do you judge yourself?

- How have you felt judged in the past, perhaps during your childhood?

- Who do you put down, or who have you put down in the past?

- When do you tend to be sarcastic or cynical?

- Do you sometimes have cruel or vindictive thoughts?

- As a child, were you ever mean or cruel to other children?

- As a child, were you ever bullied?

- What about yourself are you ashamed of?

Finding Joy in Your Golden Shadow

Happiness is an inside job.

Working with Your Golden Shadow

By now, we might have a very personal understanding of how our shadow shows up in our daily lives and affects every aspect of it. So far, in this little journey through our shadow, we have predominantly been exploring our sadness, anger and fear. These might all be considered negative aspects, and we often associate the shadow with these negative traits.

But we can also deny and suppress our good and positive parts, in what we call the Golden Shadow. The concept of the *positive* shadow might seem contradictory at first. However, just as we can repress our undesirable qualities, we can also hide away our positive attributes, especially those that weren't validated or encouraged in our childhood or social environment. These can include qualities such as creativity, spontaneity, joy, resilience and even leadership skills.

Why Do We Hide Our Joy?

Throughout our lives, various factors contribute to us losing touch with our joyful selves. Societal expectations, familial pressures or personal traumas can lead us to believe that certain positive aspects of ourselves are not acceptable or valuable. We might have learned that being too joyful, expressive or creative was not welcome. Over time, these joyful and positive parts of ourselves retreat into the shadow.

We might seek out things to give us happiness and joy in the short term, but don't last. This might include material objects such as a new car, new clothes, good food or more money. There are many examples of wealthy people who have everything they have ever wanted, and yet they are not truly happy: true happiness and joy comes from within.

EXERCISE:
Journaling on Joy

- Think back to a happy memory of when you felt truly joyful and alive. How old were you? Describe the memory.

- Write a list of things you are grateful for right now. Include small things, like a nice coffee, a sunny day and so on. You can revisit and revise this list every day.

- Reflect on the people in your life whose company you enjoy. Why you enjoy their company?

- Think of your favourite place to be, where you feel the happiest. Why do you like this place?

- Think back to your childhood or earlier years. Were there hobbies or activities you loved but have since abandoned? Why did you enjoy them? How did you feel while engaged in these activities? What might it be like to reintroduce one of these hobbies into your life now?

Building Your Self-Belief

You may have denied and suppressed many positive aspects of yourself, such as the ability to speak up and express your opinion, or the ability to play a sport. In the exercise *What's in My Shadow?* (see page 24), we looked at what we admired in others, and how this might point to an attribute in ourselves that has been denied and suppressed.

You might have a self-belief that says, 'I am not good at...', or more generally, 'I am not good enough'. This is a self-belief that you learned in your childhood. Perhaps it was the result of parents with high expectations and harsh judgements, or maybe it came from your teachers, peer group or from society as a whole.

You can react to this deep belief and fear in your shadow in two ways. Either you deflate and just accept you aren't good enough, resulting in low self-esteem and a sense of failure. Or you inflate and push yourself to achieve success and show everyone you are more than good enough. This might come with pressure to keep on driving yourself; you might start to believe there is always a higher bar to reach.

In shadow work, we aim to accept all parts of ourselves, no matter how much we have denied and suppressed them, We accept ourselves as a whole, and find affirmation that we are 'good enough' just the way we are. We cultivate a deep compassion for all parts of ourselves and come to believe that all parts of us are trying to serve us in some way. When we achieve a higher level of self-acceptance, we also achieve a higher level of contentment, giving us access to internal happiness and joy.

EXERCISE:
Meditation to Bless All Parts of Yourself

In this exercise, we welcome all parts of
ourselves. We welcome the parts we have
become more familiar with through the
exercises in this book, and any other parts
of ourselves.

Find a comfortable and quiet place to sit where you won't be disturbed. You might want to make the place relaxing, with soft lighting or candles, or maybe gentle music.

- Sit in a relaxed position, either on a chair with your feet flat on the ground, or on a cushion in a cross-legged position. Gently close your eyes and take a moment to settle into your space.

- Begin by focusing on your breath. Take deep, slow breaths, inhaling through the nose and exhaling through the mouth. With each exhale, feel yourself becoming more grounded and centred. Don't force the breath, let the body breathe naturally.

- Notice the sensations in your body: the contact points with the chair or floor, the air on your skin, any tension or relaxation in your muscles.

- Follow your natural breathing for a few minutes. If you are distracted by any thoughts, notice and acknowledge them, but gently return to the breath.

- When you feel settled, bring to mind any part of you that feels sadness. Welcome this part and invite it to be with you. Hold it gently in your mind with love and compassion.

- Bring to mind any part of you that feels anger. Welcome this part and invite it to be with you. Thank it for the work it does to protect and defend you.

- Bring to mind any part of you that feels fear. Welcome this part and invite it to be with you. Thank it for the work it does in keeping you safe.

- Bring to mind any parts of you that feel guilt or shame. Welcome these parts and invite them to be with you. Thank them for the lessons and teaching they give you.

- Finally, bring to mind any part that feels joy. Welcome this part and invite it to be with you. Thank this part for all the fun and happiness it brings you.

- Bring all the parts of you to mind, welcome them all, and invite them to be with you. Thank them all for what they have done and will do for you. Welcome them all to form the whole of you.

- Return to the breath for a few minutes, then gently open your eyes and return to the space you are in.

Conclusion

Together, through these pages, we've explored the multifaceted nature of the shadow, from its formation and influence on our lives, to various ways we can engage with and integrate it.

We've delved into deep emotional territories, examining sadness, grief, anger, anxiety, fear and the roles of our Inner Critic, Inner Child, Inner Adult, Persecutor and Safety Officer. Most importantly, we've discovered the joy and the positive aspects of our shadow – our Golden Shadow – illuminating the path to a more balanced and authentic self.

The journey of shadow work is not one that ends with the closing of this book. It is an ongoing process of self-discovery, self-acceptance and self-compassion. The exercises and reflections presented here are tools that we can return to time and again, each time gaining a little more awareness of our shadow and its impact on our lives. They are meant to guide us as we continue to explore the depths of our inner world, helping us to confront and embrace all parts of ourselves.

You may want to continue your shadow work with deep process work, facilitated by a trained shadow-work practitioner, who can help you to bring sustainable healing to your emotional wounds.

Remember, shadow work is not about reaching a state of perfection. It's about striving for wholeness. It's about acknowledging and accepting the full range of your human experience: the light and the dark. Each step you take in this work helps to illuminate the shadows, integrating these hidden parts into your conscious life. This process is not always easy, but it is profoundly rewarding.

As you move forward, carry with you the understanding that embracing your shadow is a powerful act of self-love. It's a journey that not only enhances your own life, but also allows you to bring more empathy, understanding and compassion into your relationships with others. By doing this work, you contribute to a more conscious, accepting and whole world.

Further Reading and Resources

A Little Book on the Human Shadow, by Robert Bly

Attached, by Dr. Amir Levine and Rachel Heller

How to Break Free of the Drama Triangle and Victim Consciousness, by Barry Weinhold and Janae Weinhold

TA Today: A new Introduction to Transactional Analysis, by Ian Stewart and Vann Joines

Warrior, Magician, Lover, King, by Rod Boothroyd

The author's website:
www.richardmartynhealingtheshadow.co.uk

Healing the Shadow:
www.htsorganisation.co.uk

Also available

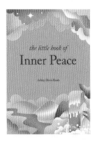

the little book of
Inner Peace

the little book of
Mindfulness

the little book of
Gratitude

the little book of
Meditation

the little book of
Tarot